A GUIDE TO

EVALUATING TEACHING

FOR

PROMOTION AND TENURE

by:

John Centra
Robert C. Froh
Peter J. Gray
Leo M. Lambert

Edited by:
Robert M. Diamond

Center for Instructional Development
Syracuse University

COPLEY PUBLISHING GROUP
LITTLETON, MASSACHUSETTS 01460

TABLE OF CONTENTS

ACKNOWLEDGEMENTS

We would like to express our appreciation to Barbara A. Yonai and Jean Young for their editorial assistance and to June Mermigos who survived the typing of numerous drafts of these materials.

INTRODUCTION

Evaluating teaching as part of the promotion or tenure process is seldom accomplished in a way that is satisfying to everyone involved. The reasons are many:

- There are often conflicting points of view about the relative importance of teaching in relation to scholarship, publication, and service.

- The criteria for judging other factors (scholarship, publication, service, etc.) are more clear cut, easier to use, and to many, more objective.

- Teaching is more complex than is generally represented by the evaluation techniques that are commonly used.

- From committee to committee there is a lack of standardization or consistency in the procedures and criteria that are used to evaluate teaching.

- A lack of communication often exists between those who are being evaluated and those who are doing the evaluation.

Despite these problems, evaluating teaching is an essential element in the promotion and tenure decision process and must be done in a manner that is fair, comprehensive, and cost effective.

Using this Manual

This booklet has one primary purpose—to help improve the process of evaluating teaching for use in tenure and promotion decisions. Whether you are serving on the promotion and tenure committee or are the faculty member being evaluated you will want the process to be fair, comprehensive, and sensitive to the particular type of teaching involved. You also want to give teaching the weight it deserves in the overall decision process.

The process for evaluating teaching should be both logical and comprehensive. Such a process provides the basic structure for this guide. It consists of three basic steps.

- Identifying the specific characteristics of effective teaching that are to be measured.

- Selecting and developing the data collection techniques that will be used to evaluate each characteristic identified.

- Implementing the evaluation—being sensitive to the instructional goals of the course and the teaching techniques being employed. This step includes data collection, analysis, interpretation, and reporting.

It is our hope that with the use of this manual, promotion and tenure decisions regarding teaching will be based on valid, reliable, and meaningful information. It is, therefore, intended for those being evaluated and those serving on promotion and tenure committees.

Being Evaluated

As a faculty member there will be a number of times during your career when you will go through the process of being formally evaluated for promotion or tenure. A key factor that will be considered is your effectiveness as a teacher. The make-up of your committee and the priorities established by your department, discipline, school, college, or institution, to a large part, will determine the importance placed on your teaching. However, no matter what the context, advanced planning on your part with respect to collecting evidence about your teaching will result in a fairer final decision.

While the evidence used to evaluate your scholarship, publications, and service is generally agreed upon and relatively easy to collect, this is not necessarily true for assessing the effectiveness of your teaching. It is up to you as the faculty member being evaluated to help provide systematically-collected data from a number of sources so that your teaching is evaluated fairly and is given the weight it deserves.

Also keep in mind that the timing of promotion and tenure decisions will be no surprise to you. You will know far ahead of time what decisions have to be made, when they will take place, and in general, the procedures that will be followed. Therefore, you have an opportunity to plan for the evaluation by collecting data now that will help you two, three, or even four years in the future.

If you wait until the last minute to collect data to support your effectiveness as a teacher you will find that you have missed many important opportunities to gather useful information. In addition, you will be forced to rely on those data collection techniques that the committee can use in the short time available to it and, if problems with your teaching are identified, you will have little time to show improvement.

For example, you might want to consider the following questions:

- Do present student ratings show problems that you can correct and then provide evidence of improvement?

- Are you designing new courses or developing instructional materials that you can evaluate for effectiveness?

- Have you tried new approaches to your teaching that have had a positive impact on improving student learning or reducing attrition and can you collect data that show the changes?

- Can you document the relationship between course objectives, course content, and student learning?

Remember, if you want to be able to show cumulative evidence of effective and improved teaching, the time to start is several years before the formal decision-making process begins.

Serving on a Promotion and Tenure Committee

As a faculty member you will not only be evaluated from time to time, but you will also serve on promotion and tenure committees. As a committee member you will have three major questions to answer in regard to teaching:

- Does our decision-making process give the appropriate weight to teaching, in relation to scholarship, publication, and service?

- Is the committee asking questions and using techniques most appropriate to the type of teaching it is evaluating?

- Is the committee collecting all the data necessary to adequately measure teaching effectiveness?

Just as you wish to be evaluated fairly yourself, you and the other members of the promotion and tenure committee will want to be fair to the faculty members you evaluate.

We work hard to ensure that the tasks of admitting students, advising students, and assessing students are based on a variety of information. We hire faculty and administrators after extensive and systematic searches that consider diverse characteristics. We judge the quality of colleagues' scholarship, publication, and service using generally-acknowledged criteria. Unfortunately, the criteria for judging teaching often are narrowly focused rather than broadly based. What is needed is the use of a number of techniques that provide information from various perspectives on different characteristics of teaching and that are sensitive to the particular teaching assignments of the faculty member being evaluated.

<u>What Should be Evaluated? Characteristics of Effective Teaching</u>

A concise, universally-accepted definition of effective teaching does not exist. But perhaps the following broad definition will provoke little disagreement:

Effective teaching produces beneficial and purposeful student learning through the use of appropriate procedures.

This definition identifies both the outcomes of effective teaching—student learning—and what the teacher does as important considerations. Therefore, both effective teaching procedures and evidence of student learning will be discussed in this section.

Wotruba and Wright (1975) summarized twenty-one studies in which groups of students, faculty members, and administrators were asked to identify qualities of effective teaching. Based on this summary we have identified the following six characteristics of effective teaching:

- Good organization of subject matter and course
- Effective communication
- Knowledge of and enthusiasm for the subject matter and teaching
- Positive attitudes toward students
- Fairness in examinations and grading
- Flexibility in approaches to teaching

For our purposes one additional characteristic, that focuses on the goal of effective teaching, is added:

• Appropriate student learning outcomes

Remember as we review each of these characteristics that (1) some are more easily measured than others, (2) faculty members will display different patterns of strengths, and a good teacher will be strong in many of these but not necessarily in all of them, and (3) that no two faculty members will be equally strong on every factor. It will be up to the committee to choose the characteristics that, for the type of teaching involved, will carry the greatest weight.

<u>Good organization of subject matter and course.</u> Good organization of the subject matter and the course itself is reflected in the objectives, course materials, assignments, class activities, and examinations. The extent to which the instructor is prepared for class and the effective use of class time are also indicators of good organization. Although everyone occasionally gets off track in terms of covering the identified course objectives, having this happen regularly can be a sign of poor organization.

In the final analysis, if a course is presented in a logically-organized and sequenced manner that promotes student learning, then it can be said to contribute to effective teaching. Of course, the inherent logic and appropriate sequence of a given course is the instructor's prerogative. Therefore, the assessment of good organization might best be made by colleagues or appropriate administrators, since they have the necessary background to understand such situations. Students can indicate their perceptions of course organization and planning, too. Students in a given class can judge with reasonable consistency (1) whether the instructor presented material in an orderly manner, (2) whether the instructor was well prepared for each class, (3) whether he or she made clear what was expected to be learned, and (4) whether or not lectures facilitated good note taking.

Course organization is particularly important to assess because research indicates that it is related to how much students learn (Centra, 1977; Cohen, 1981). Just as a well-organized textbook facilitates learning, so too does a well-organized course.

<u>Effective communication.</u> Much of the teaching in higher education—in fact the vast majority—consists of lecturing. Therefore, lecturing ability, including the

6

use of audiovisual aids or other techniques to engage student attention, is an important teaching characteristic to evaluate. Communication skills include clarity of presentation, verbal fluency, interpretation of abstract ideas, good speaking ability, and the ability to listen.

Being able to communicate the organization and sequence of a course is also an important characteristic of effective teaching. This can occur verbally through direct explanation, it can be inherent in a well-organized presentation, it can be present in a course syllabus, and it can be evident in the course materials.

Effective communication is important in large classes, seminars, laboratories, small discussion groups, as well as in one-to-one conversations. Communication skills appropriate in each of these settings is somewhat different. It is important for a faculty member to reflect on his or her communication in each setting and to develop feedback mechanisms to monitor effectiveness.

Student ratings of verbal communication, peer reviews of distributed materials, and collegial observation of actual presentations and discussions can be useful ways to gather data on effective communication. Students usually can judge with considerable accuracy such characteristics as whether the instructor spoke audibly and clearly, whether the course purposes and objectives were clearly stated, whether the major course concepts, content, and issues were clearly communicated, whether instructions for class assignments were clear, and whether the course materials used were clear and understandable. They can also determine if questions are answered clearly and if the faculty member is effective in leading small group discussions and one-on-one conferences. Of course, not every faculty member will be rated highly on all these abilities. Over time, however, faculty can gather evidence of their communication abilities in a variety of settings so that promotion and tenure review can be based on a diverse and representative set of evidence.

Knowledge of and enthusiasm for the subject matter and teaching. Faculty must know their subject matter in order to organize it in a meaningful way for students and to communicate the content that is worth knowing. In many courses it is also important that teachers present current thinking in the discipline, including recent findings from research. It may also be appropriate to present divergent viewpoints if they exist. The choice of the textbook, the readings and reference lists, the lecture content, and the course syllabus should reflect these examples of teacher knowledge of the subject matter.

Closely aligned with knowledge is enthusiasm for the subject matter. It is not enough for a faculty member to know his or her subject well; effective teaching requires that enthusiasm for the subject _and_ enthusiasm for teaching be evident. In some instances, a faculty member may know the subject well, but not communicate enthusiasm for it, or for teaching. Such situations often lessen one's effectiveness in the classroom.

Judgments about sufficient knowledge may best be made by colleagues, since they are most likely to be familiar with a given subject area. Sometimes off–campus experts are asked to judge the adequacy of a text, reading materials, and a syllabus when there is no one on campus who can form an expert opinion. Students are unlikely to have the necessary background to make these judgments, and their ratings would likely reflect whether the teacher _appears_ to know the subject matter. Although students should not judge the teacher's knowledge, they are usually aware of whether divergent views are presented.

Judgments about enthusiasm are quite subjective and are likely to differ from time to time and from person to person. The way people show or interpret a personal interest in a class or enjoyment of teaching varies considerably. Therefore, evidence about enthusiasm should be collected from students in many different courses over several semesters. When gathered in such a manner, this information can provide an added dimension to the assessment of teaching effectiveness.

Positive attitudes toward students. A favorable attitude toward students is reflected in a number of ways:whether an instructor provides help when students have difficulty with the material, whether the instructor encourages students to ask questions or express opinions, whether or not the faculty member is accessible to students outside of class and, in general, whether the instructor is aware of and concerned with what students are learning. A general atmosphere that reflects support of student learning and of a healthy student self-image are also signs of a positive attitude toward students.

All classes can have such an atmosphere although different techniques are needed to create it in a large lecture class versus a small seminar. Out-of-class accessibility can also reflect a favorable or unfavorable attitude toward students. While students are undoubtedly in the best position to judge the instructor's attitudes and actions it is important to keep in mind that some students may have unreasonable expectations that need tempering in an analysis of any data.

Some faculty members argue that what has just been described as a positive attitude toward students—providing assistance when students request it, encouraging questions, and the like—amounts to coddling students. These teachers, believe that students should dig out the answers by themselves and should not be overly dependent on the teacher to provide explanations or assistance. Without question, student effort and involvement in learning is critical, but to reject students when questions persist is certainly discouraging and reflects a lack of concern on the part of the teacher. Effective teaching involves appropriate expectations, assistance, and encouragement of students. Such teaching shows concern for students' progress in the subject matter, in their independence, and in their self-motivation.

Fairness in examinations and grading. From the very beginning of a course, students should be told how much the various course assessments, such as paper, projects, exams, and quizzes, will count toward their final grade. The relevance of each of these to the material covered in the course is a critical aspect of fairness. Consistency is essential among the goals and objectives of the course, its content, and its tests, quizzes, and assignments. Consistency is also important in regard to what is covered and its relative emphasis. The timeliness and utility of feedback regarding students' performance are also important elements of fairness, as is the equity of the workload for the credits received. Feedback in the form of grades and comments not only should be indicators of the knowledge gained relative to others in the class, but they should also be indicators of personal growth. In this way they can exemplify the instructor's positive attitudes toward students.

Fairness in grading students does not mean giving A's when they are not deserved. Studies have shown that students' assessments of the course and instruction are not dependent on getting undeservedly-high grades. Judgments of grading and examination standards can be made by selected colleagues. Colleagues and administrators can also be particularly helpful in judging whether various assessment methods reflect the course goals and objectives and whether they promote independence and higher-level thinking abilities. It is more important that the standards of grading be clear, consistent, and appropriate than that a certain percentage of every class be given A's, B's, C's, etc.

Flexibility in approaches to teaching. Faculty who try different instructional approaches are less likely to lose their enthusiasm for teaching. In addition, a variety of approaches may be useful in accomplishing a wide array of course objectives and in responding to diverse student backgrounds. Simulation and game techniques, for example, can be especially worthwhile in teaching analysis, synthesis, and critical thinking skills. Audiovisual materials can be used to supplement lectures and readings to the benefit of many students. By varying the pace of instruction for different students they can be given the time needed to master the material.

To be effective, a teacher must adapt instruction to the course content and to the students. One's first effort in this regard may not be completely successful. A willingness to experiment, based on sound feedback, can often result in a very effective course.

Flexibility in approaches to teaching may only be evident to the instructor. It is important that he or she documents the information that led to trying a different approach, the nature of the change, and the subsequent results. Colleagues and administrators can then judge the appropriateness and success of a teacher's use of different instructional techniques. This assumes, of course, that colleagues are familiar with the methods used by a teacher and the potential benefits of those methods. Information about less common methods may be included as part of the documentation.

Appropriate student learning outcomes. How much and what students learn in a course are the result of a number of factors, not all of which are teacher-related. Student ability and motivation, for example, are highly related to relative student achievement. In addition, some students may learn in spite of, not because of, the instruction in a course. Therefore, isolating the effects of teaching on learning is extremely difficult.

In spite of this difficulty, it is important to consider student learning when evaluating effective teaching. Learning outcomes can be classified as cognitive vs. affective, and low-level (e.g., the acquisition of knowledge) vs. high-level (e.g.,analysis and synthesis).[1] The process of precise classification is time-consuming and may not be worth the effort. However, it is important to ensure that student learning is consistent with the objectives established for the course. Research on college-level teaching indicates that faculty often unintentionally stress and then evaluate low-level abilities, such as recall of facts, in their examinations while doing little with the more significant and higher-level abilities.

Assessing the organization of the subject matter content will identify inconsistencies between the stated objectives and what is actually being taught. Similar assessments might also uncover inconsistencies between course objectives and what is tested for in exams and quizzes. These inconsistencies are not only confusing to students, but they also lead to an inappropriate assessment of student learning.

Student examination performance is probably the best information that can be obtained on student outcomes. Data collected at the beginning of a course can be used as a base against which to measure learning. A common final examination used in multiple section courses is useful in systematically comparing teacher effectiveness. However, examination data do have limitations for tenure and promotion relative to such questions as: Did the teacher teach to the test?; and Were students in the different sections of equal ability?

Affective learning outcomes, such as changes in attitudes and values, are more difficult to measure than subject-related knowledge, but are not impossible to measure. For example, students can be asked to reflect on the extent of changes in their attitudes and values over the semester through self-reports.

Student outcome information should be reviewed in the context of data on student attrition. Having a large proportion of the students who take the final examination reach the specified objectives is far more significant if a larger percentage of the students who started a course are still in it. A high attrition rate can be an indicator of a major instructional problem and can seriously bias student outcome information.

---

[1] Cognitive levels of learning are discussed in great detail in the well-known Taxonomy of Educational Objectives: Cognitive Domain (Bloom, et al., 1956).

11

At the conclusion of this first step, the promotion and tenure committee must decide which of these seven characteristics will be included in the overall evaluation. Some consideration must also be given as to the weight that will be assigned each characteristic. The next section focuses on the techniques that can be used to provide evidence of teaching effectiveness.

DATA COLLECTION TECHNIQUES

In this section you will find an overview of the data collection techniques that can be used to evaluate teaching effectiveness. Included are an analysis of each technique as well as discussions of its advantages and disadvantages.

Prior to collecting data, three fundamental questions must be addressed:

- Who is going to make the decision?
- What procedures and guidelines will they be following?
- What kind of evidence will the decision-makers (in this case the promotion and tenure committee and appropriate administrators) consider credible?

A Framework for Evaluation

Some departments or individual faculty members may have strong biases about a particular means of data collection. Good ideas and effort may be wasted if these biases are ignored or are not aired during constructive discussion. The Planning for Evaluation Flowchart on page 15 is intended to suggest alternative data collection techniques that can be used by various evaluators to collect information about the characteristics of effective teaching. By referring to the chart, promotion and tenure committees can ensure that important data collection methods and relevant information are not inadvertently omitted .

The chart addresses three questions: Which characteristics (of effective teaching) will be evaluated? How will data be collected, i.e., self reports, interviews, surveys, etc.? and Who will do the evaluating, i.e., oneself, students, colleagues, etc.?

The previous section of this guidebook has provided information about the first dimension of the chart, the characteristics of effective teaching. As has been suggested, one or more of these characteristics are the focus of any evaluation effort.

The second part of the chart covers data collection techniques. These are generic, common means of data collection. They include both methods (e.g., structured interviews) and instruments (e.g., instructional rating surveys). These techniques take on real form only after the evaluation focus(es) and evaluator(s) have been identified.

The "evaluators" in the third box of the chart are the individuals who will make assessments and judgments about one or more of the characteristics. In some cases, the evaluator's role also includes the responsibilities of gathering, analyzing, and interpreting data. For example, a faculty member may gather and interpret data from past student evaluations to help show how classroom communication skills have improved.

The chart is useful because it readily identifies the major evaluation focuses, common evaluation techniques, and potential evaluators. Each of the techniques is discussed in the remaining portions of this section. For each technique, the "evaluator" is identified who might logically make best use of the approach. Included is a statement of purposes, some examples of appropriate instruments, a brief review of advantages and disadvantages, and a list of suggested readings for further reference. Full references may be found on pages 47-49.

Planning for Evaluation Flowchart

Which characteristics will be evaluated?

- Good organization of subject matter and course
- Effective communication
- Knowledge of and enthusiasm for the subject matter and teaching
- Positive attitudes toward students
- Fairness in examinations and grading
- Flexibility in approaches to teaching
- Appropriate student learning outcomes

How will data be collected?

- Self-assessment/report
- Classroom observation
- Structured interview
- Instructional rating survey
- Test or appraisal of student achievement
- Content analysis of instructional materials
- Review of classroom records

Who will do the evaluating?

- Self
- Students
- Faculty
- Dean or department chair
- Alumni
- Other appropriate administrators

TECHNIQUES: SELF-ASSESSMENT/REPORT

EVALUATOR: SELF

Purpose

A <u>self-assessment</u> is an opportunity for faculty to take stock of accomplishments, long-term goals, plans, strengths, and weaknesses with regard to teaching. It is a critical self-appraisal, and requires taking time out from a hectic, demanding schedule to reflect on the process of teaching.

Formal self-assessments include checklists or survey-type instruments and written journal or log entries reflecting on teaching philosophy and pedagogy. Types of informal self-assessments include an inventory of teaching strengths and weaknesses, or simply a conversation with a trusted colleague to share ideas, plans, and perceptions of teaching successes and shortcomings.

The self-assessment is the logical first step in an individual faculty member's effort to improve his or her teaching skills and should guide future data collection activities. For example, a classroom observation could be structured to focus on a specific issue raised in the self-appraisal, such as the quality of classroom discussions. Faculty engaging in self-assessment for improvement purposes are likely to benefit from comparing their self-assessment to other sources of data, particularly student ratings. Some faculty may also benefit by discussing their self-assessment with a colleague, who may be able to challenge or support the assessment in a helpful way. It should be recognized that self-assessments do not carry much weight in the tenure and promotion process because of their subjectivity.

In contrast to a self-assessment, a <u>self-report</u> is a simple description of one's teaching activities, including numbers and names of courses taught, number of students taught and advised, service on dissertation committees, involvement with instructional development activities, and descriptions of teaching methods employed. Whereas, a self-assessment requires making judgments and evaluations of one's own performance, a self-report is a more straightforward, verifiable accounting of one's teaching-related activities.

For promotion and tenure purposes, a self-report of teaching activities is essential. For personnel decisions, most argue that self-reports should be basically descriptive, reflecting primarily on teaching philosophy, courses taught, number of advisees, involvement with curriculum development, etc. (Braskamp, Brandenburg, and Ory, 1984). Self-reports may also contain information that may explain or interpret other evaluative data.

17

Example: A Self-Assessment Form for Faculty*

The purpose of this form is to help faculty identify professional areas they would like to further develop. For each topic, faculty respond according to the scale below:

1 = NOT NECESSARY   (I don't feel that I need help in this area.)
2 = LOW PRIORITY   (I am interested, but for the time being, this
                              is a low priority.)
3 = MORE INFORMATION   (I'd like to find out more about this area.)
4 = READY FOR ACTION   (I would like to become involved in this area
                              as soon as possible.)

Good organization of subject matter and course

1 2 3 4   1. Planning my course in order to present the subject matter in a well-structured and logical manner

1 2 3 4   2. Developing my course based on a specified set of learning objectives

1 2 3 4   3. Obtaining students' feedback for purposes of course restructuring and improvement

Effective communication

1 2 3 4   4. Giving effective, well-organized lectures with clear goals and appropriate examples

1 2 3 4   5. Having students respond to questions I raise

1 2 3 4   6. Having students formulate and ask questions related to the topic

1 2 3 4   7. Having students become involved in group discussions

*Based on a form from the Office of Faculty and Instructional Development, San Jose State University. Used with permission.

Self-Assessment Form—page 2

Positive attitudes toward students

1 2 3 4 8. Establishing an atmosphere in the classroom that encourages students' receptivity to the instructional program

1 2 3 4 9. Building good rapport with the students

1 2 3 4 10. Developing sound interpersonal relationships with students in order to encourage their personal development and self-confidence

Fairness in examinations and grading

1 2 3 4 11. Using assessment techniques to measure the student's knowledge of the course content based on defined standards

1 2 3 4 12. Using assessment techniques to measure students' ability to apply their knowledge

Flexibility in approaches to teaching

1 2 3 4 13. Making use of a variety of media and resources to add interest and clarity

1 2 3 4 14. Providing opportunities for independent study and small group work

1 2 3 4 15. Designing an instructional system in which the students are pretested and guided into alternative activities (self-paced and group) to reach desired learning outcomes

1 2 3 4 16. Providing flexibility in course structure by relating it to the self-perceived needs of the students

<u>Advantages</u>

The self-report involves little formal data collection and need not consume vast amounts of time. It promotes reflection about teaching philosophy and method, and may help put other sources of data about teaching in their proper perspective. Self-assessment can be an excellent starting point in planning a comprehensive and thoughtful evaluation of teaching.

<u>Disadvantages</u>

Self-assessment is biased by its very nature, and it rarely can stand alone to provide valid evaluative data about teaching. Self-assessments are typically not useful for promotion and tenure decisions. (As has been stressed throughout this document, multiple sources of information must be sought.) Some people also find it very difficult to engage in self-critical activity, or may shy away from discussing shortcomings with colleagues.

<u>For Further Reference</u>

Braskamp, Brandenburg, & Ory (1984), pp.70-73.
Centra (1979), pp. 47-72.
Seldin (1984), pp. 147-151, 166-174.

TECHNIQUE: CLASSROOM OBSERVATIONS BY COLLEAGUES

EVALUATORS: FACULTY AND APPROPRIATE ADMINISTRATORS

Purpose

Along with student ratings of instruction, classroom observation is one of the more frequently used forms of instructional evaluation. Direct observations provide a counter point to information gathered indirectly through student rating surveys, alumni surveys, or administrator comments.

In some institutions members of the promotion and tenure committee or other faculty visit a given professor's classes and report observations in an unstructured way. Comments may be made about such items as discussion topics, mastery of content, and student interest level. Objectivity is insured by conducting a number of observations before they are used in decision making.

Other institutions have developed both a worksheet to guide observations and a process to gather information regarding teacher effectiveness. For example, a committee may be designated to conduct all classroom observations. This more structured format and process help to ensure that a full picture of the strengths and weaknesses of a given faculty member is presented.

Classroom observations are typically complemented by a number of the other techniques for observing and making judgments, particularly reviews of course materials and syllabi. This is extremely critical because (1) there is such a small number of people who are able to make observations, (2) the selection of the classes is necessarily limited, and (3) the specific characteristics focused on are a small sample of the total possible to observe. It is useful to precede any observation with a meeting between the instructor and observer to summarize course objectives and materials, and to determine areas of focus for the observation. Moreover, it is critical that as many observations as possible take place over as long a period of time as possible to increase the validity of the conclusions drawn.

Example: Classroom Observation Factors

The following items might be used to guide classroom observations. Sample items using a scaled response and open-ended questions are listed under the characteristics of effective teaching.

Good organization of subject matter and course

Scaled response items: Made a clear statement of the purpose of the lesson

Presented topics with a logical sequence

Summarized major points of the lesson

Written response question: How did the instructor demonstrate good organization of the subject matter?

Effective communication

Scaled response items: Projected voice to be easily heard

Listened to student questions and comments

Presented examples to clarify points

Written response question: What were the most and least helpful things the instructor did to communicate effectively?

Knowledge of and enthusiasm for the subject matter and teaching

Scaled response items: Presented material appropriate to the stated purpose of the lesson

Demonstrated command of the subject matter

Encouraged student involvement

Written Response Question: What content appeared to be the most and least suitable to the lesson?

Positive attitudes toward students

Scaled response items: Encouraged student discussion

Encouraged students to answer difficult questions

Used questions to determine if students were having difficulty

Written response question: How did the instructor show interest in students and their learning?

Fairness in examinations and grading

(Not possible to evaluate in a classroom observation.)

Flexibility in approaches to teaching

Scaled response items: Used appropriate instructional techniques

Made appropriate choices between presentation and discussion

Written response questions: To what degree did the instructor vary the instructional methods for the material presented?
What other methods might have been appropriate?

Appropriate student learning outcomes
(Not possible to evaluate in a single classroom observation.)

Appendix A contains an example of a "Classroom Observation Worksheet" designed to guide the observation of one class.

Advantages

Classroom observations help to complete a more concrete and real picture of the instructor than usually appears with the use of only indirect methods, such as student ratings and administrator comments. Sometimes student ratings can be inconsistent for controversial instructors or situations, and classroom observations can provide information regarding these ratings. Classroom observations also allow a more extensive focus on substantive course content issues, such as relevance and knowledge of subject matter, scholarship, and integration of topics.

Disadvantages

There are several disadvantages to classroom observation. First, faculty tend to find it threatening to implement classroom observation when they have never used the method before. As a result, this method demands considerable tact, respect, and rapport among faculty. Second, it requires considerable faculty time to ensure that the number of observations necessary to make conclusions reliable and valid are made. Third, observations for personnel decisions must be kept separate from observations for instructional improvement decisions to protect the use of this technique for either purpose. Fourth, observers tend to vary in their definitions of effective instruction making it difficult to derive consensus regarding observations. Training observers is, therefore, recommended.

For Further Reference

Braskamp, Brandenburg, and Ory (1984), pp. 63-68.
Centra (1979), pp. 73-92.
Seldin (1984), pp. 139-145, 163-166.
Appendix A - Classroom Observation Worksheet, pp. 53-56.

TECHNIQUE: STRUCTURED INTERVIEW OF UNDERGRADUATES AND
               ALUMNI

EVALUATORS: CURRENT AND FORMER STUDENTS

Purpose

Undergraduates, and to a lesser extent, alumni, are important sources of data for assessing teaching effectiveness. They may appropriately comment on the teaching effectiveness of a current or former professor. Often, their opinions, comments, and special insights will complement and "bring alive" summarized data from student rating forms. They may report about special concern shown to them by a faculty member, or may comment about exceptional classroom ability or personal advising. These "quotable quotes" add a very personal dimension to other data on teaching effectiveness. Also, if undergraduates' experience with a given professor is recent enough, they may be able to comment on specific, notable teaching behaviors that are of special concern to the promotion and tenure committee. They may also be able to comment on how well they were prepared by a given faculty member in an introductory course for upper division study in the discipline.

Alumni can offer a broad, somewhat detached perspective on the general value of their academic program and the usefulness and worth of specific courses. But because alumni ratings of a given teacher correlate highly with current students' ratings (Centra, 1979), it is usually easier and less costly to collect evaluations from current students. However, in some special cases it may be worthwhile contacting certain alumni about a teacher's effectiveness: for example, a former graduate student who worked closely with a professor on a thesis, research project, or independent study may be able to make some particularly astute observations.

Example: Structured Interview Questions

The following questions may be used in interviews with current or former students.

Sample questions for current students include:

- Describe why you would or would not recommend Professor Smith's class to a friend?

- To what extent do you believe Professor Smith's class(es) prepared you for advanced work in the subject?

- What is your overall assessment of Professor Smith in terms of:

    - course organization?
    - communication skills?
    - enthusiasm for the subject and for teaching?
    - rapport with students?
    - fairness of examination and grading practices?

- How would you describe Professor Smith in relation to other teachers you have had?

Sample questions for former students:

- What was your working relationship with Professor Smith?

- Why did you choose to work with Professor Smith?

- To what extent did the instructor provide appropriate guidance, support, and counsel?

- Please compare Professor Smith's classroom and out-of-class teaching style.

- How satisfied are you with the amount and kind of feedback provided by Professor Smith?

- What is your overall assessment of Professor Smith in terms of:

    - course organization?
    - communication skills?
    - enthusiasm for the subject and for teaching?
    - rapport with students?
    - fairness of examination and grading practices?

Advantages

The above questions are best raised in face-to-face or telephone interviews, although posing them in a letter requesting a written response is also possible. Interviews offer the opportunity to ask for clarification if a response is vague. They allow one to ask follow-up questions when a response merits additional attention. Interviews also provide an opportunity to clarify information on those specific aspects of a faculty member's teaching where the data are either missing or unclear.

Interviewing often yields information that is extremely rich and detailed, and even if conducted on a limited scale, may be worth the required investment of time. The use of an interview protocol (a question guide) based on items like those above, is recommended to make sure that each interview is conducted in a similar fashion and that all the basic issues are addressed.

Disadvantages

Interviewing current and former students is relatively expensive in terms of the time and effort needed to collect a representative sample of opinions. This is a major concern for promotion and tenure committees when decisions must be made about several faculty members in a relatively short time. Student members of promotion and tenure committees are often assigned the task of conducting interviews with other students. While there is nothing necessarily wrong with this practice, faculty should provide guidance regarding appropriate sample size and subject selection. Training in the use of the interview protocol is also necessary.

Data collection through interviews should be contrasted with other student input, such as student course ratings, to gauge its validity.

For Further Reference

Braskamp, Brandenburg, & Ory (1984), pp. 57-60, 73-75.
Centra (1979), pp. 41-42.

TECHNIQUE: STUDENT INSTRUCTIONAL RATING SURVEYS

EVALUATORS: STUDENTS

Purpose

Student evaluations of instruction are usually sought through rating surveys regarding both instructor performance and course characteristics. This form of instructional evaluation is often perceived to be the most acceptable, least threatening, and easiest to implement on a regular basis. The information is useful for both instructional improvement and personnel decision making.

Faculty often use a mix of items that focus on both the instructor and the course. Each of the seven characteristics of effective teaching can be addressed in these surveys. Items should be brief and focused. They should use response scales that are appropriate for the content of the item. Open-ended questions can generate important additional information. For example, students can be asked to list what they found most helpful or most confusing, and to make specific recommendations for improvement. Questions of this type improve the credibility of student ratings.

Faculty usually need encouragement to include optional questions that pursue one or two other teaching issues of interest to them. If they have contributed to the design of the survey, faculty feel more ownership in its results. A catalog of optional questions related to various teaching issues not only gives faculty the encouragement they need, but it also makes the final results more meaningful to them.

Example: Student Rating Form Items

The items on the next two pages might be used with the following response scale:

unsatisfactory	below average	average	above average	outstanding
1	2	3	4	5

Good organization of subject matter and course
  Being prepared for class
  Using class time appropriately
  Presenting topics with a logical progression
  Reviewing and summarizing course material

Effective communication
Communicating effectively outside of class
Varying tone to show vocal expression
Responding to student questions and comments
Presenting examples to clarify points

Sufficient knowledge of and enthusiasm for the subject
Relating new ideas to familiar concepts
Relating course content to recent developments
Sustaining students' interest in class
Demonstrating command of the subject matter

Positive attitudes toward students
Using constructive criticism
Helping students understand the material
Encouraging student discussion
Willing to listen to students' point of view

Fairness in examination and grading
Clarifying grading procedures
Designing examinations to reflect the content and emphasis of the course
Grading assignments fairly
Providing useful feedback

Flexibility in approaches to teaching
Varying instructional techniques
Using lecture versus discussion at appropriate times
Using methods that augmented readings to facilitate student learning
Using examples and illustrations

Appropriate student learning outcomes
Cognitive
Extent of intellectual challenge and stimulation
Increase in understanding of concepts and principles in this field
Increase in competence in this subject
Increase in ability to communicate clearly about this subject
Progress on instructor objectives

Affective
Increase in interest in the subject matter
Increase in confidence in ability to master course materials
Quality of effort you put into the course

Examples of complete student instructional rating forms may be found in the Appendices as follows:

Appendix B - Continuing Education Course Evaluation
Appendix C - Introductory Economics Course Evaluation - Student Questionnaire
Appendix D - Optional Questions Portion - "Intellectual Challenge" and "Quality of Student Effort"

In addition to the content of the items, the nature of the reporting is very important in the use of student instructional ratings for promotion and tenure decision making. Three different types of reports are recommended. The first report orders the items by the average response they evoke from students in the class as shown in the Item Comparison Report below. This report also compares the average response of one class (middle column) to the average response across all classes (right column). This ordering of responses from the strongest to weakest ratings gives a summary of the instructor's strengths and weaknesses. It also shows how these characteristics compare with other faculty in the same discipline.

For a given instructor, some of the abbreviated results are as follows:

| **Item Comparison Report** | | Score | |
| | | This | All |
Item		Rank	Class	Classes
1	Preparation for class	1	3.9	4.2
10	Communication outside class	2	3.6	4.0
.		.	.	.
.		.	.	.
7	Willingness to listen to students' point of view	9	3.0	3.1
5	Ability to sustain students' interest in class	10	2.9	2.6

The response scale ranged from 1 = unsatisfactory to 5 = exceptional. For Question 1, preparation for class, this instructor's average (3.9), is slightly higher than the average response to the other items for this class, but it is lower than the average across all classes. The advantages of this report are that (1) it shows, at a glance, an instructor's strengths and weaknesses as rated by the class and (2) it provides some basis for making comparisons among classes and instructors.

A second report provides frequency counts and percentages of each of the possible responses, as well as average ratings for each item. From this report, faculty can determine the amount of agreement among students regarding their ratings.

31

Frequency Distributions And Averages Of Item Responses

Item		Unsatisfactory n (%)	Below Average n (%)	Average n (%)	Above Average n (%)	Outstanding n (%)	N	Ave.
1	Preparation for class	3 (3)	0 (0)	34 (31)	45 (41)	28 (25)	110	3.9
5	Ability to sustain students' interest in class	13 (12)	30 (27)	34 (31)	21 (19)	12 (11)	110	2.9
7	Willingness to listen to students' point of view	11 (10)	23 (21)	35 (32)	32 (29)	8 (7)	109	3.0
10	Communication outside of class	2 (2)	5 (5)	46 (44)	32 (30)	20 (19)	105	3.6

The report below on the left can be used by the program administrator to compare classes. The size of each class (enrollment) and the number of students responding to the survey (n) are provided to help interpret the score and rank data. The responses are ordered from the highest to lowest average rating. This report provides a relative picture of how a given class compares with other classes in terms of student ratings. An abbreviated frequency distribution of the average scores for all classes is printed below on the right. An individual faculty member's report would identify only her or his class (e.g., PLS 101 Marks in the example below). All the other class identification information would be left blank. In this way, the specific instructor can see only their score in relation to other classes that were rated. In the example, Marks' average score of 2.3 across items is ranked 54th, that is, fifty-three classes received higher average ratings.

Course Overall Score and Rank

Course	Sec.	Instr.	n	Enrol.	Score	Rank
ABC 102	01	Lutz	98	110	3.8	1
ABC 102	02	Field	109	115	3.6	2
DEF 105	01	Stone	60	73	3.6	2
.						
.						
.						
PLS 101	01	Marks	111	125	2.3	54

All Course Score , Rank, Frequency, and Distribution

Score	Rank	Frequency	Distribution
3.8	1	1	*
3.7	0	-	.
3.6	2	2	* *
3.5	4	2	* *
3.4	6	3	* * *
3.3	9	4	* * * *
.			.
.			.
.			.
.			.
2.3	54	1	*

Advantages

Student rating surveys are one of the least threatening ways for faculty to get information about their teaching. Faculty typically have more control over the format and substance of student evaluations than they do over other forms of instructional evaluation. They also are more easily implemented than other techniques faculty use to get feedback on a regular basis. Optional items can be added easily to explore areas of specific interest or problems. Comparative data can be provided to give faculty an idea of their ratings relative to their peers. Survey results can be analyzed to determine differences in ratings by types of students (e.g. majors versus non-majors, expected grade, sex, prior interest). Keep in mind that student rating surveys can provide information useful for course improvement if they are administered at midterm.

Disadvantages

Student rating surveys tend to evoke very lenient responses from students so that faculty often obtain overly positive ratings. The need for comparative data in making personnel decisions encourages the comparison of ratings across faculty and courses that may have very different characteristics (e.g., differences in subject matter, experience, teaching methods). In addition, the surveys may be standardized to a point that the questions do not reflect the essence of any particular instructor's teaching style. Finally, legal issues could surface regarding the appropriateness of comparing an instructor's responses to responses obtained by peers rather than to some standard of what is determined to be an acceptable rating.

For Further Reference

Braskamp, Brandenburg, and Ory (1984), pp. 35-54.
Centra (1979), pp. 17-46.
Doyle (1983), pp. 27-42, 111-121.
McKeachie (1986), pp. 273-294.
Seldin (1984), pp. 133-139, 158-161.
Appendix B - Continuing Education Course Evaluation, pp. 57-58.
Appendix C - Introductory Economics Course Evaluation - Student
          Questionnaire, pp. 59-61.
Appendix D - Optional Questions Portion - "Intellectual Challenge" and "Quality
          of Student Effort," p. 63.

TECHNIQUE: CONTENT ANALYSIS OF INSTRUCTIONAL MATERIALS

EVALUATORS: FACULTY AND APPROPRIATE ADMINISTRATORS

Purpose

Most teachers routinely produce a number of documents and non-print materials that may reflect the quality of thought and effort they put into teaching. Included are syllabi (indicating content and/or teaching objectives), examinations and quizzes, reading lists, class assignment lists, student manuals, slides and overhead transparencies, computer programs, and student advising documents. Other documents produced by students, such as theses, papers, and other projects, also may reflect the quality of guidance and supervision provided by faculty outside of the classroom. Faculty colleagues' critiques of these materials are likely to provide a perspective on teaching abilities not obtainable through other means, such as classroom observations.

Peer review of written material for promotion and tenure should be both formal and systematic. Faculty may be required to assemble a portfolio of materials for review. Departments may wish to draft a checklist or protocol to guide the critique of the portfolio by at least two reviewers who are familiar with the candidate's content area. (The candidate also may be given an opportunity to respond to the critiques.) Reviewers outside of the candidate's department may provide an objective point of view, although they will, of course, be unfamiliar with the course content.

Example: Content Analysis Questions

The following list includes questions that might be used to guide the analysis of instructional materials relative to the characteristics of good teaching.

Good organization of subject matter and course
  Does the content appear to be appropriate and relevant?
  Is the content appropriately sequenced and paced?

Effective communication
  Are the course goals and objectives clearly stated?
  Are student assignments well-defined?
  Are grading standards and performance expectations well-defined?

Knowledge of and enthusiasm for subject matter and teaching
Are texts and other sources appropriate for the course?
Does the reading list reflect careful selection of sources?
Are reading requirements appropriate?

Fairness in examinations and grading
Do examinations promote critical thought and analysis?
Are the question types (essay, multiple choice, etc.) appropriate for the content and consistent with what was taught?
Are grading standards applied fairly and consistently?
Are the exam questions clear and well thought-out?
Do examinations test course objectives?

Flexibility in approaches to teaching
Do the course materials suggest creativity and flexibility by including a variety of instructional approaches (e.g., lectures, debates, discussions, field trips, games/simulations, movies/video tapes)?
Are student assignments and projects varied, and can they be tailored to individual student's interests when appropriate?
Are other innovative methods employed to encourage faculty-student contact, such as "networking students" and teacher on a computer system to pose and respond to questions, make assignments, etc.?
Have teaching materials, such as student manuals, study guides, and instructional media been produced? What is their quality?

Appropriate student learning outcomes
Do student papers, theses, and projects reflect superior guidance and support from the faculty member?
Does the faculty member make insightful comments about students' work? Does he/she encourage students to excel?
Are student-produced documents consistent with the course goals and objectives in regard to the course content and level of learning?
Is there evidence that teaching materials enhance teaching and learning?

Advantages

There are several strengths to this technique. The fact that written products such as syllabi and examinations are submitted for evaluation as part of a portfolio may help to raise quality standards. The technique itself is one of peer review, which many faculty value and respect. Also, the technique provides a relatively rare chance to share a tangible product related to teaching with colleagues. This alone may help to promote, within the department, more frequent discussions about effective teaching.

Disadvantages

The idea of including peer reviews of teaching-related documents and non-print materials is appealing because of the straightforward nature of the technique. However, the process could be troublesome in a department where personal relationships among faculty are poor. This problem could be offset by including peers from outside the department in the review process.

For Further Reference

Braskamp, Brandenburg, and Ory (1984), pp. 68-69.
Centra (1979), pp. 73-92.

TECHNIQUE: REVIEW OF CLASSROOM RECORDS

EVALUATORS: SELF, OTHER FACULTY, DEANS/DEPARTMENT CHAIRS

Purpose

An often overlooked source of evaluative data for making decisions about teaching are common institutional records, such as records of: grades, student retention data (by course), students taught (or advised) per semester, and students who have chosen to take two or more classes from the same faculty member. If this information is collected over time, faculty may discover significant trends. For example:

- A faculty member has a significant percentage of students from an introductory survey course who subsequently elect to enroll in one of his/her advanced courses.

- An instructor's grade distributions appear to be very odd—a very high percentage of both A's and F's.

- Almost one-third of the students in a professor's sophomore-level "core curriculum" course drop out and must repeat the course at a later time.

One or more of these examples could provide very misleading information without supporting data from other sources. For example, in the third example above, the professor may continually have a large number of students enroll in a class who are not prepared to perform well in a competitive curriculum. This relatively large attrition rate may not be due to a teaching problem, but may instead reflect the need to reexamine admissions standards or the freshman curriculum. Other institutional records may be useful in further defining this problem. For example, high school records and data examining freshman performance in prerequisite courses may indicate specifically how students are underprepared.

Institutional record data may also be useful in signaling successes in teaching. Reduction in attrition in major courses or greater student preparedness for advanced coursework may indeed be the result of a faculty members' hard work and attentiveness to effective teaching. Again, data from other sources must be used to support claims of special impact.

For promotion and tenure decisions, faculty may wish to provide their committee with a summary of relevant data. Besides basic information such as numbers of students taught and advised as described under Self-Assessment/Report, faculty may wish to list students who have opted to enroll in two or three of their courses. Faculty may also choose to provide commentary on grading practices (if warranted) and to provide background data on students that may help put anomalous situations into perspective.

Names and ID numbers of students who have
taken two or more of my elective courses:

1. Mark Goldman   127-94-8222
2. Sarah Grace   111-44-6666
3. Bill Little   062-18-9191

% of my Freshman students who have three
or more years of High School Math

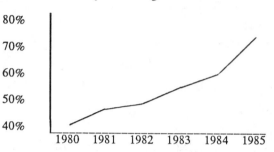

Advantages

Longitudinal classroom records are relatively easy to collect and maintain. Copies of enrollment forms and grade lists are routinely available to faculty. Even "unofficial" background data on students (reported by students) can be collected on three by five cards. For example, faculty may wish to poll students about such information as their majors, preparation in the subject area, high school background, and areas of interest, in order to informally monitor trends that may help interpret other data on teaching effectiveness.

Disadvantages

Individual faculty and personnel committees should be cautious not to jump to the most obvious explanation of enrollment or grading trends. A faculty member who gives a large percentage of A's is not necessarily teaching a "gut" course or giving simple exams. (A review of the teacher's syllabus and examinations will shed some light on this situation.) Conversely, a faculty member whose class size is 35% smaller in December than it was in September may be neither on ogre nor a bore. Other data must be used to explain atypical situations.

For Further Reference
Braskamp, Brandenburg, and Ory (1984), pp. 75-76.

Based on the previous discussion it may seem we are suggesting that (1) all faculty should rate highly on all of the characteristics influencing effective teaching, (2) as evaluated by every possible person, and (3) using all the techniques available. This is clearly impossible because of several factors. The first is the natural diversity among faculty and their teaching situations. The second is the limitations on resources that are available for evaluating teaching. The third is the usually tight time-schedule for making promotion and tenure decisions. There are, however, some ways that the impact of these factors can be minimized.

Individual faculty members and groups of faculty have different opinions about (1) the relative importance of the various characteristics that influence effective teaching and (2) how the characteristics might be expressed in a given area (e.g., writing class, biology section, philosophy course, art studio, chemistry lab., physical education course). While all faculty should have acceptable ratings in all characteristics, patterns of exceptionality will differ. Individual faculty should identify their particular strengths and build on these to ensure acceptable ratings in all other areas. Groups of faculty (e.g., programs, departments, colleges) should identify minimum standards for teaching, based on the characteristics. In addition, they can develop illustrative profiles of exceptional capability that provide guidance to individual faculty on ways to excel in teaching.

In order to identify strengths and weaknesses, and to make necessary improvements, faculty should begin collecting data about their teaching at the earliest possible date using a variety of techniques. This will help to off-set any limitations in these areas that are part of the promotion and tenure process itself. For example, it is usually impossible to show improvement over the short period of time that teaching is evaluated as part of the promotion and tenure decision-making process. In addition, the limited resources available at that time may mean that only one or two methods can be used to evaluate teaching. However, over a four-year or five-year period a faculty member can collect a number of evaluations from a variety of people (e.g., students, colleagues, administrators, and himself/herself) using several different techniques (e.g., instructional rating surveys, guided observations, and self–assessment/reports). Not all available people or every possible technique need be used. However, if multiple perspectives are represented, and if there is consistency among the data collected, then evidence will be more credible and will more likely show the impact of changes in teaching over time.

Promotion and tenure committees should set standards for acceptable ratings on the characteristics and they should determine how to identify exceptional capability appropriate in a given area. Written guidelines describing the characteristics and the techniques previously used to gather information about them might be included in a faculty handbook. In addition, by encouraging faculty to begin collecting a variety of data early in their careers, promotion and tenure committees can offset the typical lack of resources and tight timelines associated with the promotion and tenure process.

Another way to facilitate the inclusion of diverse data on teaching is to form a "committee on teaching" to collect and evaluate all pertinent evidence regarding a candidate's teaching. Typically, it is the responsibility of the faculty to collect and make available to the committee information related to his/her teaching. This information may include course syllabi, past student evaluations, instructional materials, etc. The "committee on teaching" may seek additional information through interviews, classroom observations, and letters from previous students. Committee members would then summarize this information and provide an overall assessment of the candidate to the promotion and tenure committee. In effect, the use of a "committee on teaching" increases the resources available to evaluate teaching and, because it works parallel with the promotion and tenure committee, it can provide information within the usually brief timeline for decision making.

In summary, the nurturing of good teaching must come from individual faculty, administrators, and promotion and tenure committees all working together. Because teaching is a complex and very personal activity, its evaluation must be tailored to the individual being evaluated and the discipline in which the teaching takes place. Therefore, there is no one technique or source of information that can provide the definitive assessment of teaching capability. The best solution to this dilemma is to:

- use a variety of techniques that
- gather information from different people,
- over a long enough period of time,
- to be able to document with reasonable confidence,
- the quality of teaching, and
- the impact of any changes that have been made to improve instruction.

REFERENCES

Blackburn, R.T., & Clark, M.J. (1975). An assessment of faculty performance: Some correlates between administrator, colleague, student, and self-rating. Sociology of Education, 48(2), 242-256.

Braskamp, L.A., Brandenburg, D.C., & Ory, J.C. (1984). Evaluating teaching effectiveness. Beverly Hills: SAGE Publications, Inc.

Centra, J.A. (1983). The fair use of student ratings. Postsecondary Education Newsletter.

Centra, J.A. (1979). Determining faculty effectiveness. San Franciso: Jossey-Bass.

Centra, J.A. (1977). Student ratings of instruction and their relationship to student learning. American Educational Research Journal, 14(1), 17-24.

Centra, J.A. (1976). Faculty development practices in U.S. colleges and universities (PR-76-30). Princeton, N.J.: Educational Testing Service.

Centra, J.A. (Winter 1976). The influence of different directions on student ratings of instruction. Journal of Educational Measurement, 13(4), 277-282.

Centra, J.A. (1975). Colleagues as raters of classroom instruction. Journal of Higher Education, 46(1), 327-337.

Centra, J.A. (1974). The relationship between student and alumni ratings of teachers. Educational and Psychological Measurement, 34(2), 321-326.

Centra, J.A. (1973). The effectiveness of student feedback in modifying college instruction. Journal of Educational Psychology, 65(3), 395-401.

Centra, J.A. (1973). Self-ratings of college teachers: A comparison with student ratings. Journal of Educational Measurement, 10(4), 287-295.

Centra, J.A., & Creech, F. R. (1976). The relationship between student, teacher, and course characteristics and student ratings of teacher effectiveness (PR-76-1). Princeton, N.J.: Educational Testing Service.

Cohen, P.A. (1981). Student ratings of instruction and student achievement: A meta-analysis of multisection validity studies. <u>Review of Educational Research</u>, <u>51</u>, 281-309.

Costin, F., Greenough, W. T., & Menges, R. J. (1971). Student ratings of college teaching: Reliability, validity, usefulness. <u>Review of Educational Research</u>, <u>41</u>,(5), 511-535.

Doyle, K.O., Jr. (1983). <u>Evaluating teaching</u>. Lexington, MA: D.C. Heath and Company.

Doyle, K.O., Jr. (1975). <u>Student evaluation of instruction</u>. Lexington, MA: D.C. Heath and Company.

Druckers, A.J., & Remmers, H.H. (1951). Do alumni and students differ in their attitudes toward instructors? <u>Journal of Educational Psychology</u>, <u>42</u>(3), 128-143.

Dunkin, M., & Biddle, B. (1984). <u>The study of teaching</u>. New York: Holt, Rinehart, and Winston.

Eble, K.E. (1977). <u>The craft of teaching: A guide to mastering the professor's art</u>. San Francisco: Jossey-Bass.

Educational Testing Service. (1975). <u>Comparative data guide for the student instructional report (1975-1976)</u>. Princeton, N.J.: College and University Programs.

Feldman, K.A. (1976). The superior college teacher from the students' view. <u>Research in Higher Education</u>, <u>5</u>, 243-288.

Festinger, L.A. (1957). <u>Theory of cognitive dissonance</u>. Evanston, Ill: Row, Peterson.

Green, T. F. (1971). <u>The activities of teaching</u>. New York: McGraw Hill.

Marsh, H.W., Fleiner, H., & Thomas, C.S. (1975). Validity and usefulness of student evaluations of instructional quality. <u>Journal of Educational Psychology</u>, <u>67</u>(6), 833-839.

McKeachie, W.J. (1986). <u>Teaching tips: A guide book for the beginning college teacher</u>. (8th edition). Lexington, MA: D.C. Heath and Co.

Patton, M.Q. (1980). <u>Qualitative evaluation methods</u>. Beverly Hills: SAGE Publications, Inc.

Seldin, P. (1984). <u>Changing practices in faculty evaluation</u>. San Francisco: Jossey-Bass.

Sullivan, A.M., & Skanes, G. R. (1974). Validity of student evaluation of teaching and the characteristics of successful instructors. <u>Journal of Educational Psychology</u>, <u>66</u>,(4), 584-590.

Wotruba, T.R., & Wright, P.L. (1975). How to develop teacher-rating instrument: A research approach. <u>Journal of Higher Education</u>, <u>46</u>(6), 653-663.

APPENDICES

Appendix A

Classroom Observation Worksheet

Instructor _____   Course _____

Date _____   Observer _____

Directions: Below is a list of instructor behaviors that may occur within a given class or course. Please use it as guide to making observations, not as a list of required characteristics. When this worksheet is used for making improvements to instruction, it is recommended that the instructor highlight the areas to be focused on before the observation takes place.

Respond to each statement using the following scale:

not observed	more emphasis recommended	accomplished very well
1	2	3

Circle the number at the right that best represents your response. Use the comment space below each section to provide more feedback or suggestions.

Content Organization	not observed 1	more emphasis recommended 2	accomplished very well 3
1. Made clear statement of the purpose of the lesson	-1-	-2-	-3-
2. Defined relationship of this lesson to previous lessons	-1-	-2-	-3-
3. Presented overview of the lesson	-1-	-2-	-3-
4. Presented topics with a logical sequence	-1-	-2-	-3-
5. Paced lesson appropriately	-1-	-2-	-3-
6. Summarized major points of lesson	-1-	-2-	-3-
7. Responded to problems raised during lesson	-1-	-2-	-3-
8. Related today's lesson to future lessons	-1-	-2-	-3-

Comments:

Presentation	not observed 1	more emphasis recommended 2	accomplished very well 3
9. Projected voice so easily heard	-1-	-2-	-3-
10. Used intonation to vary emphasis	-1-	-2-	-3-
11. Explained things with clarity	-1-	-2-	-3-
12. Maintained eye contact with students	-1-	-2-	-3-
13. Listened to student questions and comments	-1-	-2-	-3-
14. Projected nonverbal gestures consistent with intentions	-1-	-2-	-3-
15. Defined unfamiliar terms, concepts, and principles	-1-	-2-	-3-
16. Presented examples to clarify points	-1-	-2-	-3-
17. Related new ideas to familiar concepts	-1-	-2-	-3-
18. Restated important ideas at appropriate times	-1-	-2-	-3-
19. Varied explanations for complex and difficult material	-1-	-2-	-3-
20. Used humor appropriately to strengthen retention and interest	-1-	-2-	-3-
21. Limited use of repetitive phrases and hanging articles	-1-	-2-	-3-

Comments:

Instructor - Student Interactions	not observed 1	more emphasis recommended 2	accomplished very well 3
22. Encouraged student questions	-1-	-2-	-3-
23. Encouraged student discussion	-1-	-2-	-3-
24. Maintained student attention	-1-	-2-	-3-
25. Asked questions to monitor students' progress	-1-	-2-	-3-
26. Gave satisfactory answers to student questions	-1-	-2-	-3-
27. Responded to nonverbal cues of confusion, boredom, and curiosity	-1-	-2-	-3-

	not observed 1	more emphasis recommended 2	accomplished very well 3
28. Paced lesson to allow time for note taking	-1-	-2-	-3-
29. Encouraged students to answer difficult questions	-1-	-2-	-3-
30. Asked probing questions when student answer was incomplete	-1-	-2-	-3-
31. Restated questions and answers when necessary	-1-	-2-	-3-
32. Suggested questions of limited interest to be handled outside of class	-1-	-2-	-3-

Comments:

Instructional Materials and Environment

	not observed 1	more emphasis recommended 2	accomplished very well 3
33. Maintained adequate classroom facilities	-1-	-2-	-3-
34. Prepared students for the lesson with appropriate assigned readings	-1-	-2-	-3-
35. Supported lesson with useful classroom discussions and exercises	-1-	-2-	-3-
36. Presented helpful audiovisual materials to support lesson organization and major points	-1-	-2-	-3-
37. Provided relevant written assignments	-1-	-2-	-3-

Comments:

Content Knowledge and Relevance	not observed 1	more emphasis recommended 2	accomplished very well 3
38. Presented material worth knowing	-1-	-2-	-3-
39. Presented material appropriate to student knowledge and background	-1-	-2-	-3-
40. Cited authorities to support statements	-1-	-2-	-3-
41. Presented material appropriate to stated purpose of course	-1-	-2-	-3-
42. Made distinctions between fact and opinion	-1-	-2-	-3-
43. Presented divergent viewpoints when appropriate	-1-	-2-	-3-
44. Demonstrated command of subject matter	-1-	-2-	-3-

Comments:

45. What overall impressions do you think students left this lesson with in terms of content or style?

46. What were the instructor's major strengths as demonstrated in this observation?

47. What suggestions do you have for improving upon this instructor's skills?

Appendix B

Continuing Education Course Evaluation

Please respond to questions 1 - 4 by circling the letter that best represents your response.

1. Campus affiliation: A. University College   B. Main Campus

2. Student Status: A. Non-matriculated B. Matriculated

3. Sex: A. Male   B. Female

4. Age: A. 18-22   B. 23-30   C. 31-40   D. 41-50   E. over 51

For questions 5 - 22, use the following scale by circling the number to the right that best represents your response.

unsatisfactory	below average	average	above average	outstanding
1	2	3	4	5

Please omit any item that does not apply to your course.

	unsat	ba	ave	aa	outst
5. Clarity of course requirements	1	2	3	4	5
6. Clarity of grading system	1	2	3	4	5
7. Logical progression of course topics	1	2	3	4	5
8. Appropriate use of class time	1	2	3	4	5
9. Fairness of grading procedures	1	2	3	4	5
10. Usefulness of text and additional readings in learning the subject matter	1	2	3	4	5
11. Usefulness of audiovisual and other instructional materials	1	2	3	4	5
12. Instructor's presentational skills	1	2	3	4	5
13. Instructor's enthusiasm for teaching	1	2	3	4	5
14. Ability of instructor to relate new ideas to familiar concepts	1	2	3	4	5
15. Instructor's use of challenging questions	1	2	3	4	5
16. Instructor's use of constructive criticism and suggestions	1	2	3	4	5

		unsat	ba	ave	aa	outst
17.	Willingness of instructor to give help to students	1	2	3	4	5
18.	Instructor's openness to different points of view	1	2	3	4	5
19.	Ability of instructor to incorporate student's experiences and opinion into coursework	1	2	3	4	5
20.	Instructor's responsiveness to the needs of adult, part-time students	1	2	3	4	5
21.	Course effectiveness in increasing your understanding of concepts and/or skills in the field	1	2	3	4	5
22.	Course effectiveness in stimulating your interest in the field	1	2	3	4	5

For questions 23-30, please use the response scale provided if the instructor provides additional optional questions.

	unsat	ba	ave	aa	outst
23.	1	2	3	4	5
24.	1	2	3	4	5
25.	1	2	3	4	5
26.	1	2	3	4	5
27.	1	2	3	4	5
28.	1	2	3	4	5
29.	1	2	3	4	5
30.	1	2	3	4	5

For questions 31-32, please write your response in the space provided below the question. Attach extra paper if more space is needed.

31. What did you like best about this course?

32. What changes would you make to improve this course?

Appendix C

Introductory Economics Course Evaluation

Student Questionnaire

Some of the items below require you to respond by indicating a number between one and five. A one (1) represents <u>N</u>ot at All, a three (3) represents <u>S</u>omewhat, and a five (5) represents <u>V</u>ery Much. Others ask you to respond with either Yes (1) or No (2).

Please circle the response that most accurately represents <u>your</u> feelings.

<u>The Course Objectives</u>   N   S   V

1. To what extent has your teaching assistant listed the
   objectives at the beginning of each class?.................................. 1 2 3 4 5

Please indicate the degree to which:

2. the objectives helped you follow the lecture.............................. 1 2 3 4 5
3. the objectives helped you study the material outside of class............ 1 2 3 4 5
4. the objectives helped you understand the purpose of the
   course guide... 1 2 3 4 5

<u>The Student Course Guide</u>

5. Do you own a copy of the course guide? .... 1 = Yes   2 = No

If yes, please indicate the degree to which:

6. you used the course guide 1 2 3 4 5
7. the course guide helped you to understand the course goal.............. 1 2 3 4 5
8. the course guide helped you prepare for quizzes and exams............. 1 2 3 4 5

<u>Math Instructional Review</u>

9. To what degree did the math used in the course cause you difficulty?. 1 2 3 4 5
10. Did you complete any of the math review modules located in the
    Learning Center?... 1 2 3 4 5

If yes, for those modules which you completed, please indicate to what degree they were helpful. Leave any you did not complete blank.

11. Basic Math... 1 2 3 4 5
12. Algebra.. 1 2 3 4 5
13. Geometry 1 2 3 4 5

<u>Teaching Assistants</u>

Please indicate the degree to which you perceive your teaching   N   S   V
assistant as:

14. prepared... 1 2 3 4 5
15. organized.. 1 2 3 4 5
16. understandable in terms of level of presentation 1 2 3 4 5
17. understandable in terms of language................................. 1 2 3 4 5
18. being open to questions 1 2 3 4 5
19. treating students with respect....................................... 1 2 3 4 5
20. in control of the class.. 1 2 3 4 5
21. enthusiastic 1 2 3 4 5
22. answering questions effectively..................................... 1 2 3 4 5
23. caring about the subject 1 2 3 4 5
24. making students interested in the subject........................... 1 2 3 4 5
25. providing high quality instruction.................................. 1 2 3 4 5
26. motivating you to perform well in this course....................... 1 2 3 4 5

Course Information
Please indicate the degree to which:

		N	S		V
27. the pace of instruction was about right		1	2 3	4	5
28. the workload required was about right		1	2 3	4	5
29. the text was useful		1	2 3	4	5
30. the course material was relevant to your major		1	2 3	4	5
31. the course material was relevant to career preparation		1	2 3	4	5

Testing
Please indicate the degree to which:

		N	S		V
32. the questions to the exam were fair		1	2 3	4	5
33. the grading on the exam was fair		1	2 3	4	5
34. the exam questions covered what was taught		1	2 3	4	5
35. time to complete the exam was sufficient		1	2 3	4	5
36. the feedback was returned in a timely manner		1	2 3	4	5
37. the short quizzes or graded homeworks were useful		1	2 3	4	5

Demographic Information
Please respond to the following items so that we may better structure the course to the needs of the enrolled students. All of the information you provide will remain anonymous.

38. Circle the appropriate response.   1 = Male   2 = Female

39. What is your academic classification: (Circle one classification.)

    1 = Freshman   2 = Sophomore   3 = Junior   4 = Senior

40. Why did you enroll in this course? (Circle one response.)

    1 = Arts & Sciences required course   2 = Arts & Sciences elective

    3 = Professional school requirement   4 = Professional school elective

    5 = Other (Please specify) _____

41. Please indicate the degree to which this course motivated you to major in economics (1 = Not at all, 3 = Somewhat, 5 = Very much)

    N   S   V
    1 2 3 4 5

42. What percentage of class sessions did you attend? (Circle one response.)

    1 = less than 50 percent   2 = 51-80 percent   3 = 81-100 percent

Comments and Suggestions

43. Please note what you think are the major <u>strengths</u> and <u>weaknesses</u> of this course. Also, note <u>what</u> you would change in the course and <u>how</u> you would change it.

    Strengths:

    Weaknesses:

    What you would change and how would you change it?

44. Please use the space below to make any additional comments or suggestions about this course.

Thank you for your assistance!

CID (5/87)

Appendix D

Optional Questions Portion

These questions have been included at the option of instructors in two selected schools.

Optional Questions Regarding "Intellectual Challenge"

Rate the instructor on each of the items listed below, using the following five-point rating scale:

unsatisfactory 1	below average 2	average 3	above average 4	outstanding 5

	unsat	ba	ave	aa	outst
11. Provided intellectual challenge.	1	2	3	4	5
12. Provided new viewpoints.	1	2	3	4	5
13. Conducted discussions to evoke high quality participation.	1	2	3	4	5
14. Encouraged independent thought.	1	2	3	4	5
15. Encouraged students to think through and follow-up on material presented.	1	2	3	4	5
16. Motivated excellent work.	1	2	3	4	5
17. Stimulated intellectual curiosity.	1	2	3	4	5
18. Identified the central issues involved in the course material.	1	2	3	4	5

Optional Questions Regarding "Quality of Student Effort"

Please rate your success as a student in this course in comparison to other students by using the scale below.

unsatisfactory 1	below average 2	average 3	above average 4	outstanding 5

	unsat	ba	ave	aa	outst
16. Amount you have invested in this course.	1	2	3	4	5
17. Amount of energy you put into relating new concepts to previously learned concepts.	1	2	3	4	5
18. Participation in class discussions.	1	2	3	4	5
19. Quality of questions you asked in class.	1	2	3	4	5
20. Studied on a regular basis.	1	2	3	4	5
21. Separated important points from details.	1	2	3	4	5
22. Selected critical ideas from teacher cues.	1	2	3	4	5